SUNDAY'S CHILDREN

is a gift
to

_____

from

_____

SUNDAY'S CHILDREN

by
James Bitney
and
Suzanne Schaffhausen

SUNDAY'S CHILDREN

by
James Bitney
and
Suzanne Schaffhausen

Published by
Resource Publications, Inc.
160 E. Virginia St. #290
San Jose, CA 95112

Distributed in Canada by
Claude Primeau & Associates, Ltd.
Oakville, Ontario

Editorial Director: Kenneth Guentert
Production Editor: Scott Alkire
Mechanical Layout: Agnes Hou
Cover Design: Suzanne Schaffhausen

ISBN 0-89390-076-1
Library of Congress Catalog Card Number 86-060172
Printed and bound in the United States 5 4 3 2 1

Copyright © 1986 by Resource Publications, Inc. All rights reserved. For reprint permission, write Reprint Department, Resource Publications, Inc., 160 E. Virginia St. #290, San Jose, CA 95112

Scripture texts on pages 1, 27, 39, 51 are taken from the *New American Bible*, copyright © 1970 by the Confraternity of Christian Doctrine, Washington, D.C. Used by permission of the copyright owner; all rights reserved. Scripture text on page 15 is taken from *The Jerusalem Bible*, copyright © 1966 by Darton, Longman & Todd, Ltd. and Doubleday & Company, Inc. Used by permission of the publisher.

Sunday's Child
is bonny and bright,
filled with joy,
God's own delight.

Contents

Foreword i

1. **Sunday Is Gathering Day** 1
   Tapping Shoes 2
   Just Desserts 4
   Family Tree 6
   Signs and Wonders 8
   The Best Part 10

2. **Sunday Is a Storytelling Day** 15
   Once Upon a Time 16
   Stories 18
   Namecalling 20
   Tall Tales 22
   Laps 24

3. **Sunday Is a Thanking Day** 27
   Be Polite 28
   For Bread 30
   Nervous Eyes 32
   The Tops 34
   Whispers 36

4. **Sunday Is a Sharing Day** 39
   A Person Who Shares 40
   Bathtubs 42
   Questions 44
   Even Stephen 46
   Promises to Keep 48

5. **Sunday Shapes All Other Days** 51
   Prayer for Sunday Morning 52
   Prayer for Sunday Evening 54
   Morning Prayer 56
   Table Prayer 58
   Evening Prayer 60
   Sunday Song 62

Foreword

On my first reading of this delightful array of children's prayers, I thought, "How I wish we had this twenty years ago when our children were young." On second reading I thought, "Nonsense. These prayer-poems speak to the child in all of us."

That's what makes them so special. Parents can read them with children without feeling foolish. The feelings expressed are universal and the words are comfortable everyday ones. Missing is that awkward pious language which puts so many parents off in praying with children or talking with them about God.

I see many possible uses for this little book. Children can be invited to choose one prayer to read to the family during family prayer time. Parent and child can read one together each evening at bedtime.

Families can act the prayers out, particularly with children too young to read, by having Mom or Dad do the reading and the kids the acting. And, of course, parents can reach for a particular prayer to use to fit a child's immediate experience, as in "Just Desserts," the prayer about young friends quarreling, separating and feeling the need to reconcile.

A most valuable use, I believe, is utilizing the prayers to initiate family sharing and communication. After reading "Stories," children and grownups can share their favorite story about God or Jesus, tell who they would like to have been in scripture, choose their favorite miracle, tell when they would most like to have lived in biblical times.

In "Tall Tales," children can share their own grandparents' stories — the ones they most love to hear about Mom and Dad. In "Namecalling," the family can make a list of the names each most and least likes to be called and post it on the refrigerator.

When I direct a family retreat, I set aside time for families to write their own prayer, using their names, pets' names, and family situations. It's a popular activity and families take the prayer home with them to use weekly during family prayer time. Some print or needlepoint it and display it as their very own prayer. This book will help families with ideas and confidence in getting started comfortably in devising such prayers.

Often I am asked by parents, "But how can we learn to pray together without sounding foolish?" A variety of prayer-poems like this is a wonderful start. Thanks, Jim Bitney, for helping families and children talk comfortably to and about God.

Dolores Curran

Sunday Is Gathering Day

Sunday is a gathering day
   for Christians everywhere.
Sunday gathers all of us
   for praise and thanks and prayer.

*On the first day of the week...
we gathered for the breaking of the bread.*
                            Acts 20:7

Here are some gathering prayers
to help you get ready to celebrate Sunday.

Tapping Shoes

If I wear my Sunday tapping shoes,
I can't go play and stuff,
because the bottoms are too slippery,
and the tops will get all scuffed.

My mom says when I wear them,
they really give me poise.
But I just like to wear them
because they make a tapping noise.

Saturday night I polish them, God,
until they shine with style.
So, at Sunday church, you'll know it's *me*
tapping up the aisle.

Just Desserts

God,
Yesterday I threw a snowball
   and yelled at my friend, Bert.
The snowball missed, but not my words,
   so his feelings got real hurt.

Today Bert walked to school alone.
   He used to walk with me.
And later, Bert laughed right out loud
   when I fell and skinned my knee.

Mom said, "You got your just desserts."
   What that means, I'm not sure.
I just know that Bert and I
   are not the way we were.

I told Bert I was sorry,
   but I think he still feels mad.
Bert wouldn't even look at me,
   so I came away real sad.

Please help me get my friend back, God.
   I'm lonely, and it hurts.
I'm hungry for his friendship,
    and I'm tired of just desserts.

Family Tree

God,
we got this picture of a big tree
hanging in our living room.
The names of my great,
great grandparents
are on the trunk of the tree.
I never knew them,
but I'm sure you do,
because they're in heaven now.

A big bunch of branches
grow up and out of the tree trunk.
Each branch has a name on it.
I don't know all those names either,
but my mom and dad told me
that they're all in the family.

If you squint your eyes and look real close,
at the tip-top of the tree,
out on a tiny limb,
you'll find my name, God.
My mom and dad said I'm part of the family,
too.

But if it's not too much bother,
I was wondering something, God.
Would you mind keeping an eye on me?
My name looks pretty lonely.
And it would make me feel safer
knowing you're out on that limb with me.
Thanks, God.
Amen.

Signs and Wonders

You hear all our prayers, God, don't you?
You listen to prayers, am I right?
Well, I was kind of wondering,
Do you *see* my prayers in the night?

When my room is dark at nighttime,
And I pray with my sister, Dee,
She says you hear what she's saying,
But do you *see* the prayers from me?

I do not pray with my voice, God.
I pray with my hands and fingers, see?
I pray that way because I'm deaf
And can't hear like my sister, Dee.

I can't hear sounds like words or songs,
Not even noises like thunder.
So, prayers I pray are signs, not sounds.
Do you see them, God, I wonder?

Mom says you gather *every* prayer
And don't set signs from words apart.
Dad says you *see* *and* hear my prayers,
Because you listen with your heart.

You must be a God of wonders!
You must be a God of signs, too!
Your loving heart sees my sign prayers,
And you hear how much

I love you.

Amen.

The Best Part

God, every two weeks
we pile in the car
and go to Grandma's house.
But that's not the best part.

My dad drives and tells jokes.
Us kids sing songs,
and my mom gives us candy or gum.
But that's not the best part.

We ride on a twisting road
that follows a sparkling, little creek.
And where the creek runs into a big river,
we zoom across a tall bridge
and sometimes honk the horn.
But that's not the best part.

Then we go by a place where they make trucks,
a movie house with blinking lights,
and a fancy store with a stuffed toy octopus
hanging in the window.
But that's not the best part.

Finally we get to Grandma's house.
She's always waiting on the front porch,
wearing all her pretty rings
and her apron with the big red tulips.

Grandma opens her apron
and scoops us up in a hug.
Her apron smells like cookies and perfume
and feels all cozy and snuggly.
And even though we're family
and visit her twice a month,
Grandma makes everyone feel
just like the guest of honor.
And *that's* the best part.

Sunday Is a Storytelling Day

Sunday is a story day,
   the day good news is heard.
Sunday's stories fill us up
   with God's exciting word.

...remember the marvels (God) has done.
Psalm 105:5

Here are some storytelling prayers
to help you get ready to celebrate Sunday.

Once Upon a Time

Dear God,
I really like "once upon a time" stories.
They paint magic worlds behind my eyes.
Dragons and witches live there,
but so do lords and ladies.
In "once upon a times" I pretend
I'm a tiger in the jungle,
or a princess in a castle,
or a knight in shining armor.
I get to be like grownups
and have lots of fun.
Thank you, God, for "once upon a times"
and all the times in between.
Like you, they help me live
happily ever after.
The end.
Amen.

Stories

God of stories,
when I grow up,
I want to be a storyteller.
I want to write exciting adventures.
I want my words to make people
smile and gasp and cheer.
I know that you are a storyteller, God.
Your stories are really exciting.
I bet that's because your word is Jesus
and because Jesus is a living word.
Help me write stories
that are alive like yours.
Fill all my words with excitement.
And help me always to remember
the story of Jesus,
the greatest story
ever told.
Amen.

Namecalling

"It's not nice to call people names."
That's what I've been told, God.
But the stories I hear about you
call you plenty of names.
I remember some of them:
Lover, Shepherd, Father, Holy,
Way, Gate, Light, Lord,
Son, Spirit, Counselor, King.
That's why when I talk to you,
I sometimes like to call you different names.

When I feel lonely,
I like to call you "Best Friend."
If I get scared of something,
I might call you "Mom."
When I have hard things to do,
I call you "Helper."
And when I'm really happy,
I might call you "Joy."

I hope you don't mind it
when I call you names.
It's just my way of saying,
"I think you're special."
Amen.

Tall Tales

"Your Grandpa tells tall tales."
At least that's what Grandma says.
"Oh no, I don't," says Grandpa,
"I only tell short stories."
When he says that, God,
Grandma laughs.
I guess it's supposed to be funny.

All I know is, Grandpa tells great stories
about the olden days.
Some are sad.
Some are funny.
But his stories about Dad are best,
like when my dad wore braces
and was scared of the dark like me.

Grandpa's tales and stories
make me feel like I was in them,
like the time Dad tied the worms in knots
so they wouldn't get away!
Or the time when he made breakfast
with seven dozen eggs.

I bet you'd like Grandpa's stories, too, God,
the funny and the sad,
the tall and the short.

Laps

Guess what, God?
Guess what you have only when you're sitting
and lose when you stand up?
Your lap!
Pretty good joke, right?
I like laps a lot.
Laps can hold children and pets.
Laps are great places
to sit,
to watch TV,
to feel at home.
Laps are the coziest places
to hear scary stories
or to listen to soft songs.
Thanks for laps, God.
They're the best seats in the house.
Amen.

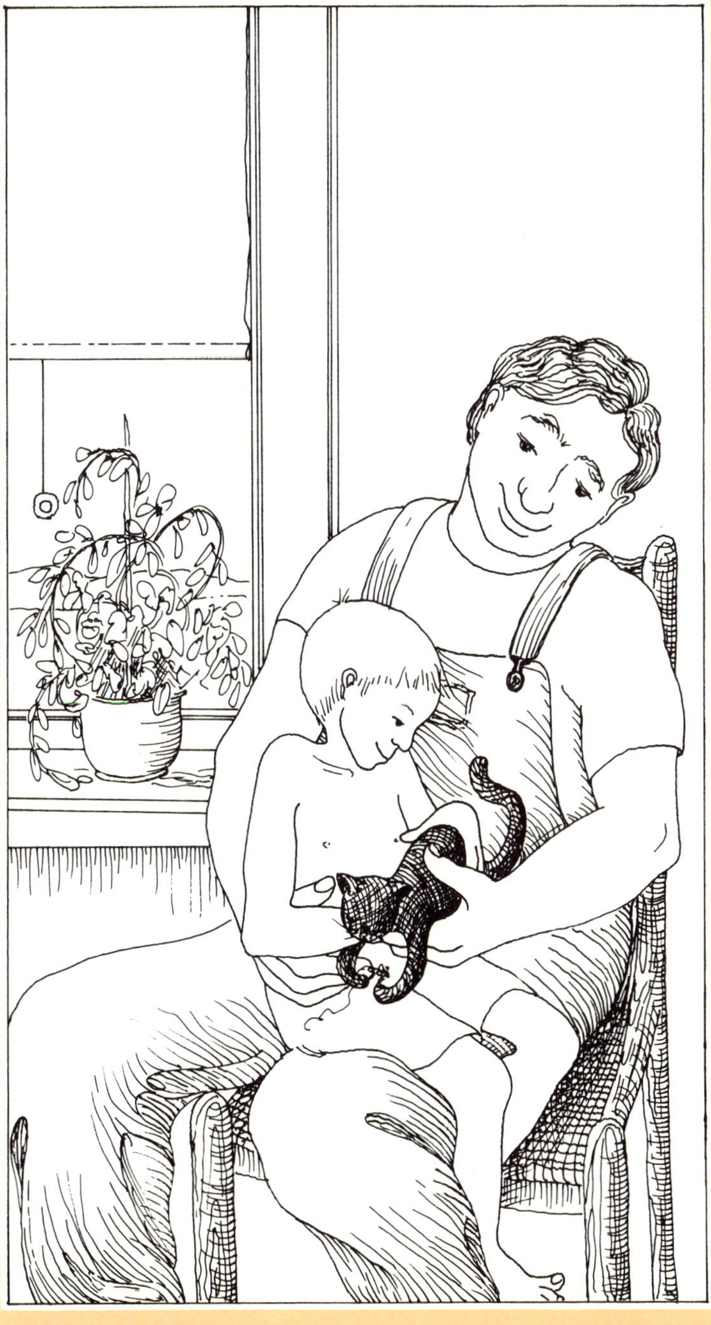

Sunday Is a Thanking Day

Sunday is a thanking day,
 for all that God has done.
Sunday gives God special thanks
 for Jesus, God's own Son.

*It is good to give thanks to the LORD,
to sing praise to your name, Most High...*
                    Psalm 92:2

Here are some thanking prayers
to help you get ready to celebrate Sunday.

Be Polite

"Now, be polite,"
my mom tells me,
"and be sure to say thank you."
But, God, it's awfully hard
to say thank you
when you get a bow tie
for your birthday
or when your aunt gives you
a real wet kiss.
It's hard to be polite
to your big sister's boyfriend
when he's always patting you on the head
and calling you shrimp or short stuff.
And sometimes I just forget,
especially if I get excited
when I get real neat presents.
So if I forget to thank *you*, God,
for all the neat things you give me,
I hope you know
I don't mean
to be impolite.
Thanks.

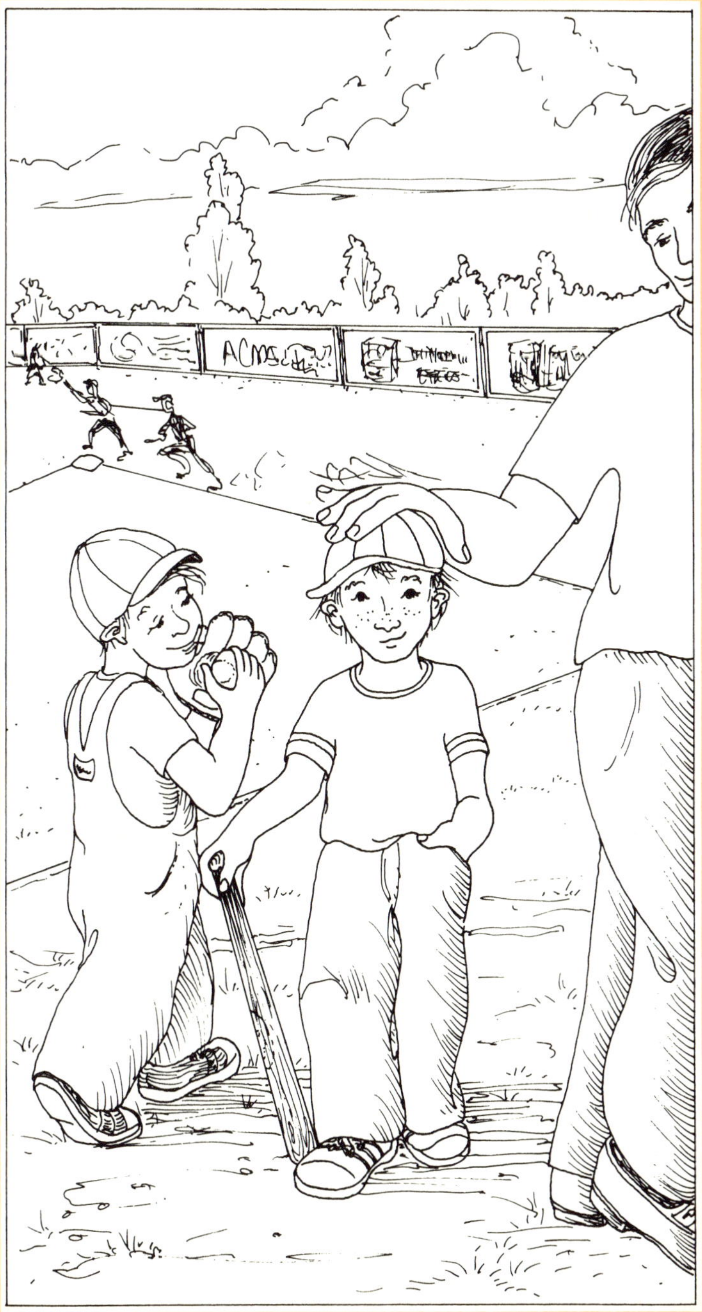

For Bread

For many grains, crushed and ground,
For sifted flour, mixed round and round,
For springy dough I love to knead,
For crunchy loaves on which to feed,
For baking bread's sweet home sweet smell,
For bread's rich taste I like so well,
For bread to break and bless and share,
The bread that shows how much you care,
I thank you, loving God.
Amen.

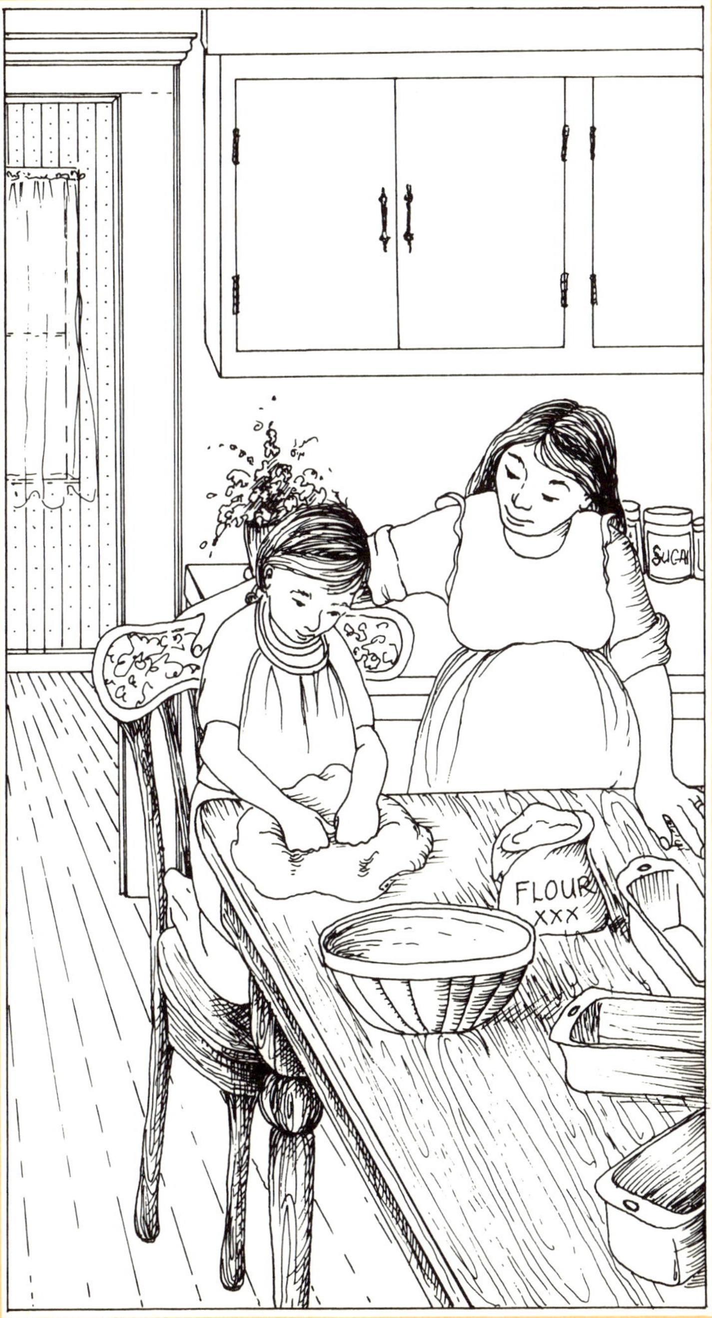
FLOUR
XXX

Nervous Eyes

When my pet mouse, Lucy, had babies,
she had six of them, God.
They were so tiny
I could fit them all in my hand
without even one of them falling out!

Once,
when I was holding them,
Lucy looked at me with nervous eyes.
But I knew she trusted me.

My mom says that you hold the sun,
the moon, the stars, the earth,
and all the people in your hand
without even one of them falling out!

Wow!
Hold onto us tight!
And even if some people look at you
with nervous eyes,
I want you to know, God,
I trust you.
Amen.

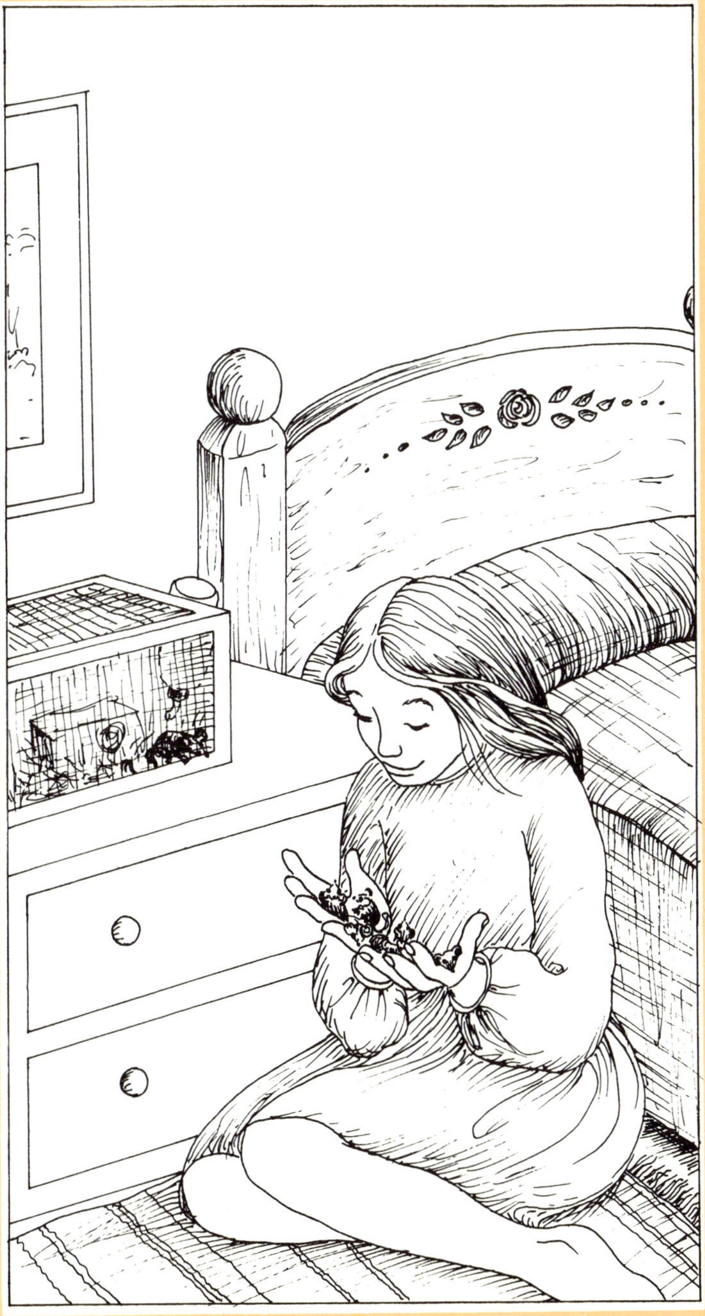

The Tops

This is a list of things I like,
    as you can plainly see.
I bet you'd like to hear it, God,
    for you gave these things to me.

I like the rain when it hits a tin roof.
I like magicians who disappear, "Poof!"

I like to slurp up real long spaghetti.
I like to sleep with my old, beat-up Teddy.

I like the purring of my friend's cat, Tanya.
I like the smell and taste of lasagna.

I sort of like snowboots — the ones without buckles.
I like the sound when I crack my knuckles.

I like to go on the rides at the fair.
I like foot-long hotdogs you can get there.

I like peanut butter spread on my toast.
I think I might like to get scared by a ghost.

I like to sing in my bedroom at night,
especially after mom turns out the light.

I like my grandpa, my frog, and my folks.
I like my teacher when she tells us jokes.

I like the feel of the silk on my blanket.
And I liked my sailboat, till my sister sank it.

I like my grandma's sweet 'tater pie.
I especially like my P-U-P-P-Y.

I like so very many things,
   I could go on and on.
But I don't want to bore you, God,
   or bother you too long.

I hope you know there's lots of things
   I like that I have missed.
I hope you know I like you, too.
   In fact, you top the list.

Whispers

Lots and lots of neat things happened today, God.
First of all, there were bananas in the cereal
and cinnamon on the toast.
When I got to school, we had a movie
instead of math.
At recess I won at ships across.
At lunch I had chocolate milk.
We *didn't* have a spelling test,
and no homework either.
After school, Pop let me come in the barn
right when he was milking.
And later he let me sit on his lap
and steer the tractor all by myself.
We had pizza for supper,
strawberry shortcake for dessert,
and it wasn't my turn to wipe the dishes.
Then I beat my brother twice in checkers
and got to stay up a whole hour late!
Now it's bedtime.
My mom said,
"No more talking, young lady,"
and she made me promise to be real quiet.
So I hope you can hear me whisper, God,
"Psst, thanks a lot!"
Amen.

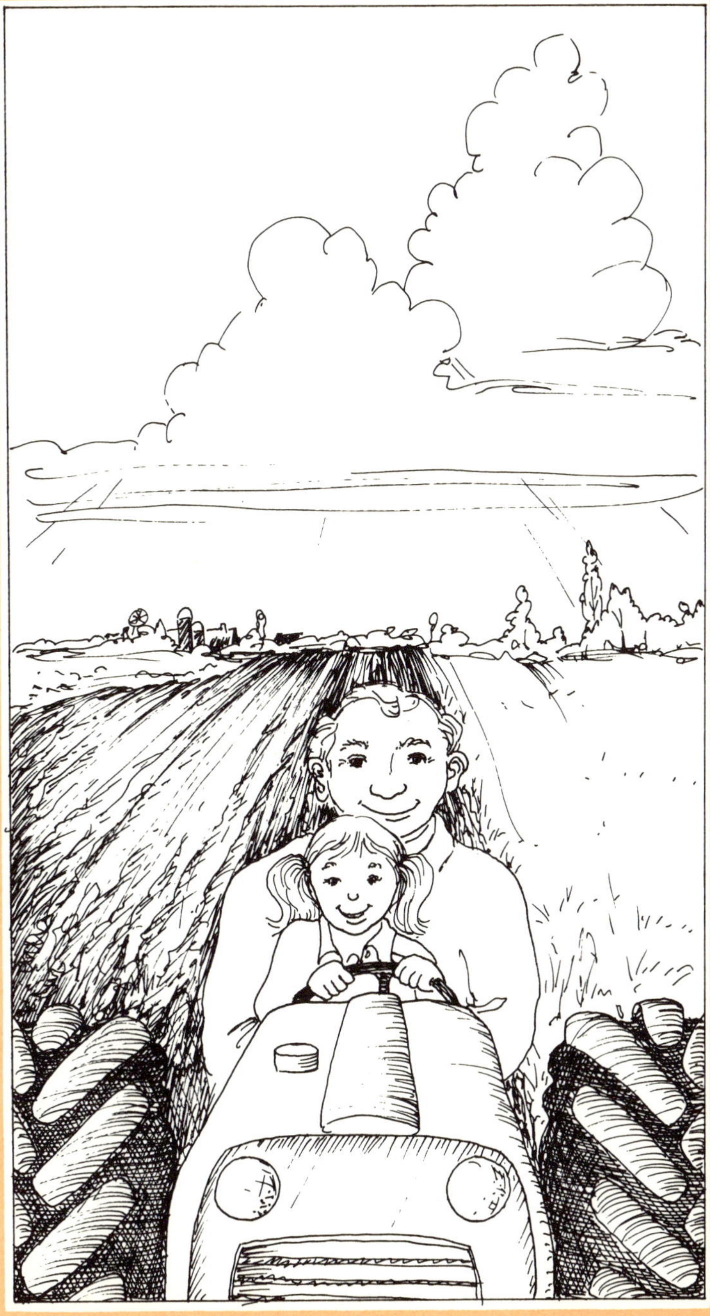

Sunday Is a Sharing Day

Sunday is a sharing day
   in life that Jesus won.
Sunday is the day we share
   the meal that makes us one.

...there was rejoicing over the great feast of the Lord in which they shared...and the children joined in, and the rejoicing...could be heard from afar off.
                            Nehemiah 12:43

Here are some sharing prayers
to help you get ready to celebrate Sunday.

A Person Who Shares

God, help me to be a person who shares,
a person who helps, a person who cares.

Help me be giving in all that I do.
Help me to grow ever closer to you.

Teach me to help the best way that I can
with wide open heart and hard working hands.

Please listen, dear God, to my simple prayer,
and help me become a person who shares.

Amen.

41

Bathtubs

When I was just a little kid, God,
I didn't like taking baths.
But later, I got used to them.
Now baths aren't so bad.
The best way to take a bath
is to fill the tub way up,
slide in the deep end,
and float with the soap.
The water makes me feel real bouncy,
like a dolphin splashing in the sea.
Sometimes I start splashing, too.
Then before you know it,
the bathtub's overflowing.

I know it sounds funny, God,
but I think that sharing is a lot like bathtubs.
You might not like it much at first,
but it's not too hard to get used to.
I especially like sharing
when you get all filled up
with ideas and important things to tell about.

When that happens,
you get to feeling real bouncy,
and before you know it,
you're overflowing!
Sharing and bathtubs
are both like that.
Right, God?

Questions

When people are nasty or hurting or bad,
do you get discouraged, God, or ever feel sad?

Do you ever get scared or nervous or hurried?
Do you ever feel troubled or tired or worried?

When people don't pray, or they act really rotten,
do you ever feel lonely, glum, or forgotten?

I'm asking these questions, God, not to intrude.
I'm not trying to pry or be nosy or rude.

But when things make you weary
or make you feel blue,
I just want you to know, God, I'll share them with you.

Amen.

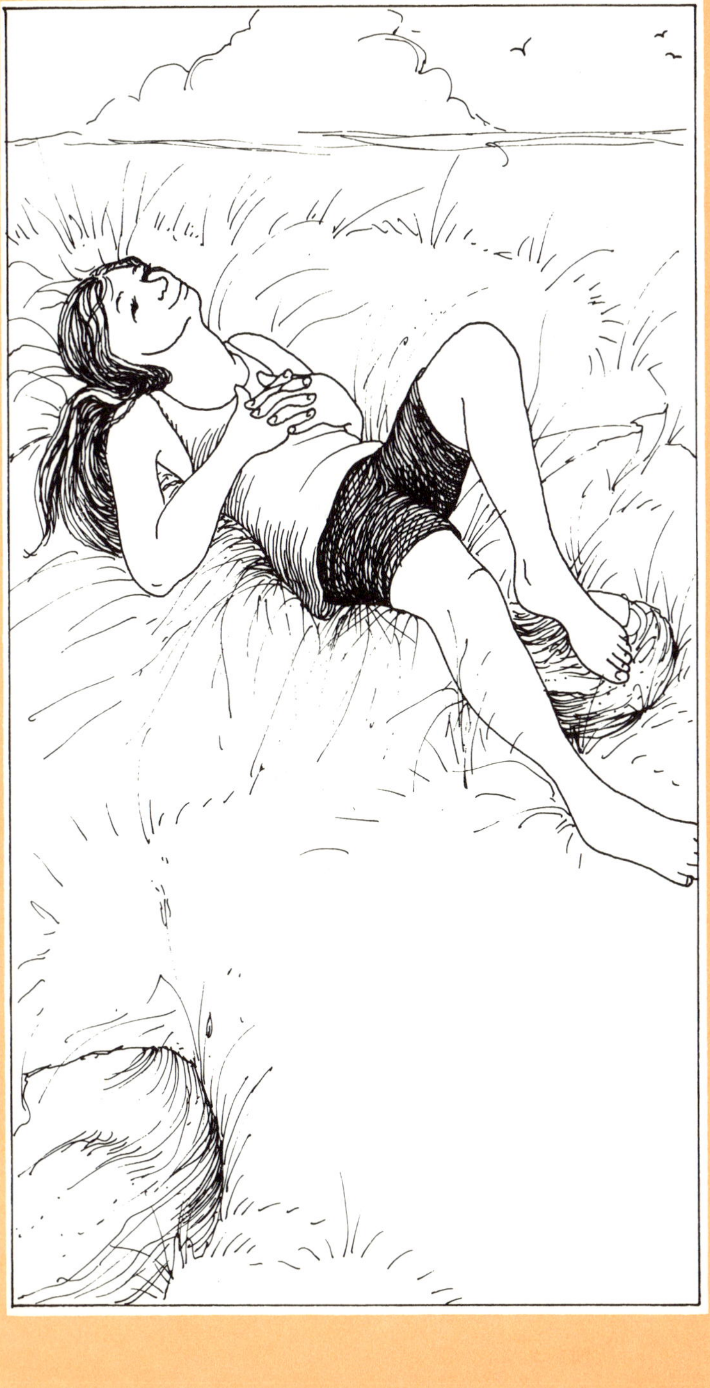

Even Stephen

Do you know what, God?
Do you know what the hardest thing
in the whole world to do is?
Well, it's when you're sharing with someone,
and you're trying to break a candy bar in half
even stephen.
It never works.
One part's always bigger than the other
or has more nuts in it.

I asked my mom to explain this,
and she told me not to worry about it.
She said that the sharing is all that matters
even if it's not always
even stephen.
But then she said I should always give
the biggest part away.
Is she right about that, God?

It doesn't sound too even stephen to me.

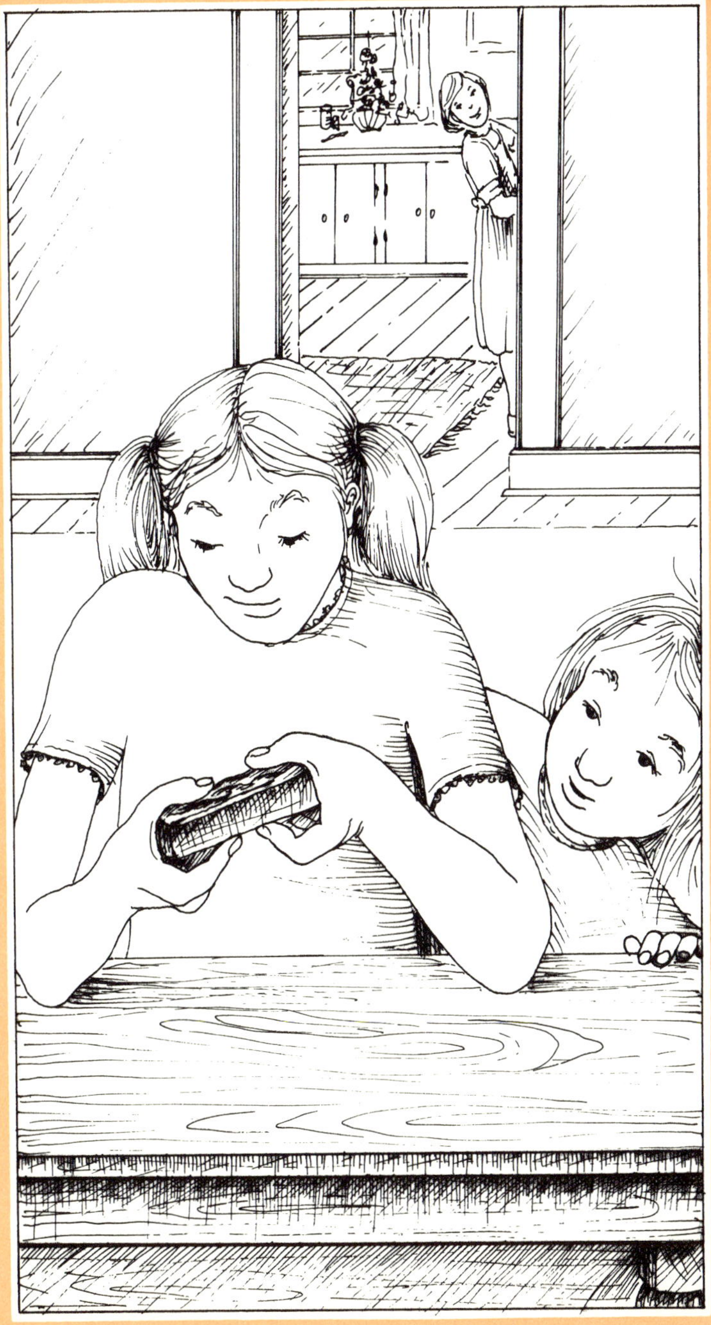

Promises to Keep

You loved us so much, God,
    you sent us your Son
to keep all your promises,
    each single one.

You know that I love you
    and love Jesus, too.
So here are some promises
    I'll keep to you.

I promise not to whine
    when I can't do what I please.
And I'll eat all my vegetables,
    even the peas.

I'll try to be nicer
    to my little sister.
Oh, I did that already, God.
    I even kissed her!

I'll clean up my bedroom
    and help do the dishes.
I'll remember to feed
    my gerbil and fishes.

I'll try not to nag,
   or to be a big pest.
My parents will like that.
   They need the rest!

I'll do all my homework
   to get ready for class.
I'll study my spelling
   and hope that I pass.

I'm sure there are promises
   I may have missed.
But you've got to admit, God,
   they make quite a list!

I know that some promises
   will be hard to keep,
and with such a big list,
   I may be in too deep.

So I saved one last promise
   in my promises rhyme.
I promise to work on them
   one at a time.

Sunday Shapes All Other Days

Sunday shapes all other days
 and sets the whole world free.
Sunday is the special day
 God gives to you and me.

*This is the day the LORD has made;
let us be glad and rejoice in it.*
Psalm 118:24

Here are some prayers
to help you live Sunday all week long.

Prayer for Sunday Morning

God,
every week
on a special day
we gather
in a special way.
My family joins with others
to hear your holy word,
to remember how you give us life,
to give thanks for what we've heard.
We share the gift of Jesus,
the meal that makes us one.
Then we go to live out Sunday's joy,
the joy of your own Son.
Amen.

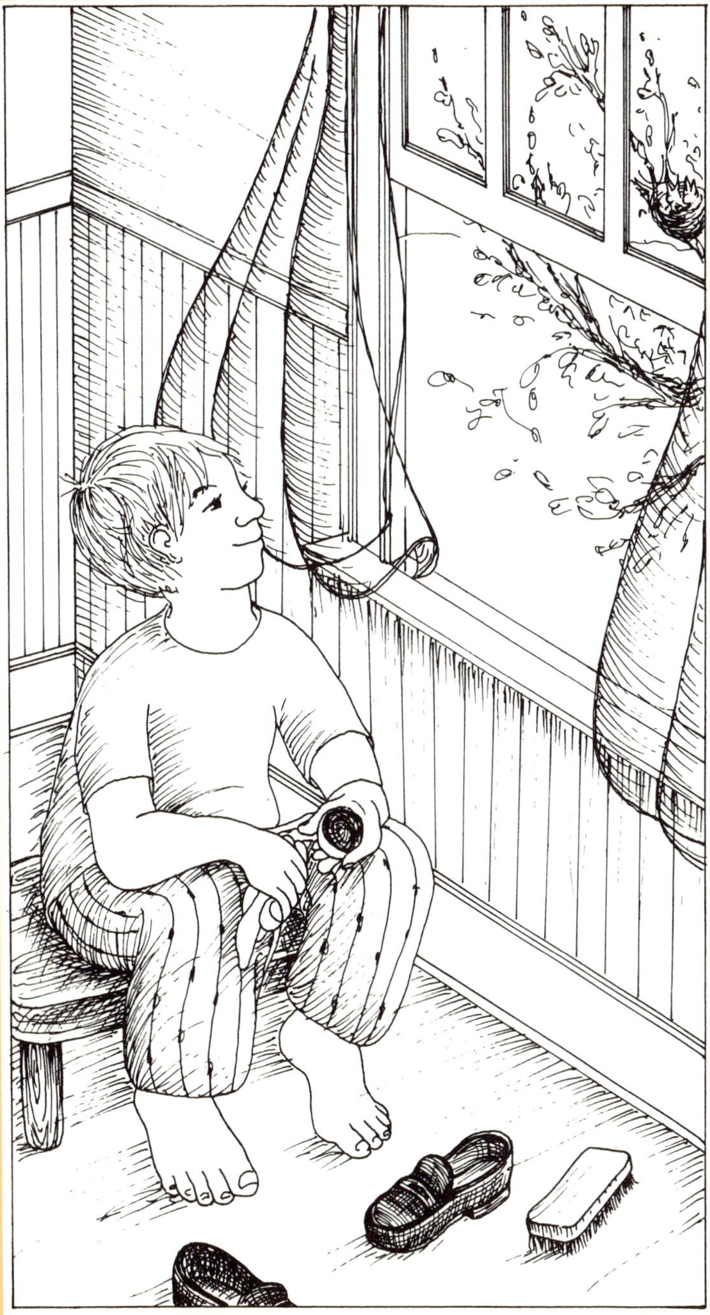

Prayer for Sunday Evening

I praise you, God, for Sunday!
You give me this day
to share with all others
in worship and play.
It is now Sunday evening;
and as shadows grow deep,
I say, "Thank you for Sunday!"
as I fall asleep.
Amen.

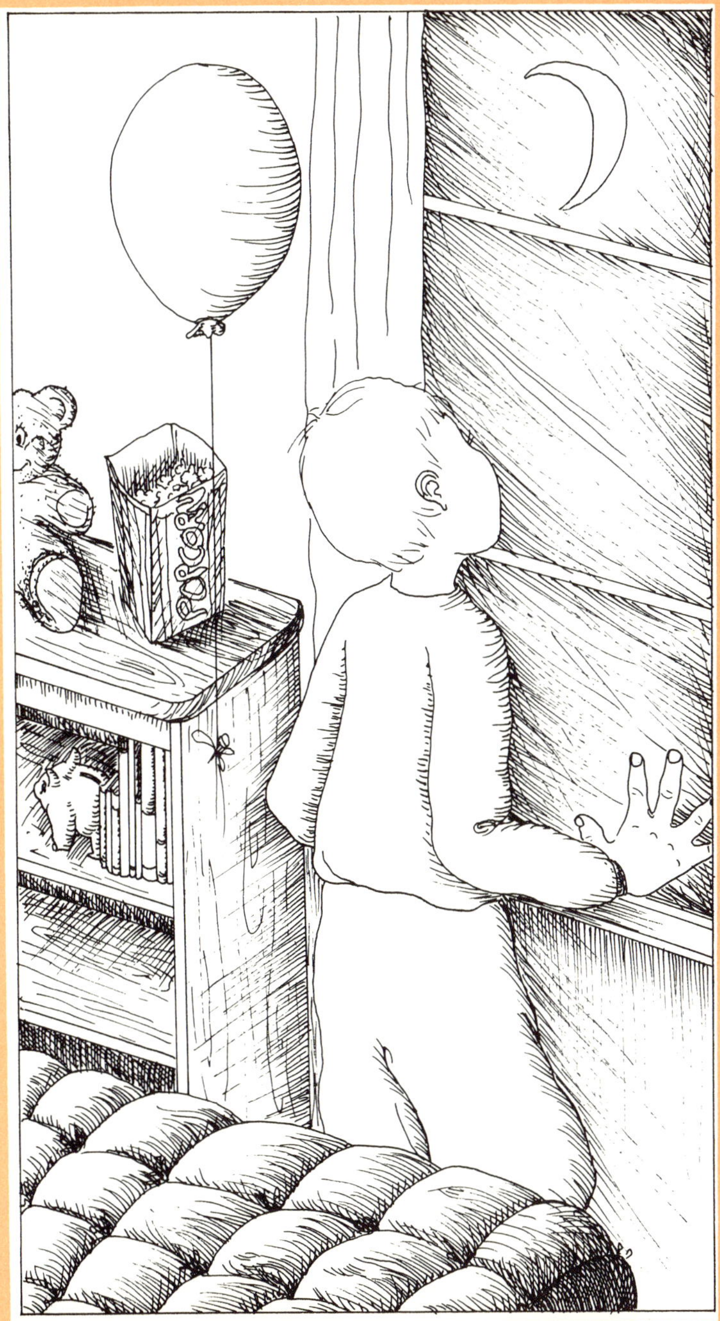
POPCORN

Morning Prayer

I praise you, God, for morning!
You give me this day
to share with all others
in work and in play.
Thank you, God.
Amen.

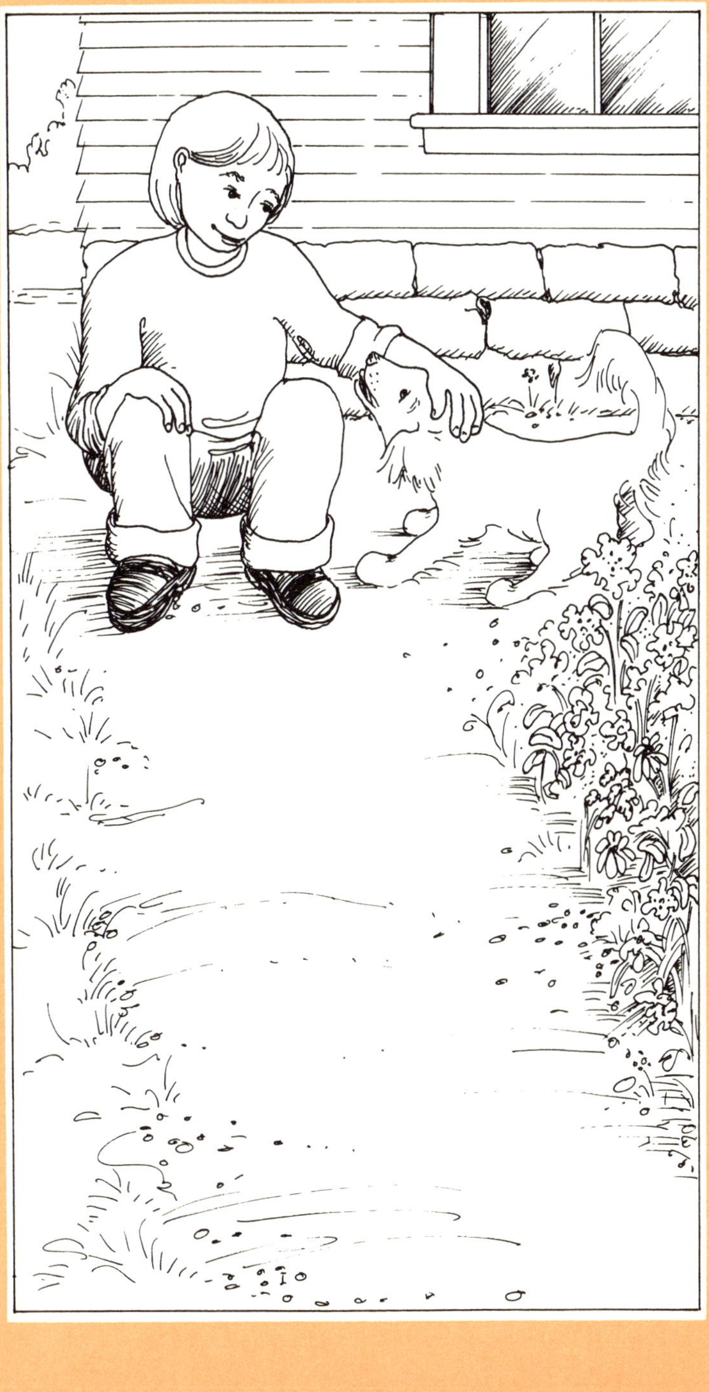

Table Prayer

We bless your name and praise you, God,
  with this our table prayer.
We thank you for the fellowship
  and food that we will share.

With bounty set our table, God.
  With affection set the mood.
Then season all with blessings rich
  to flavor all our food.

And may this time together feed
  our love as family,
that we may learn you are the God
  of hospitality.

Amen.

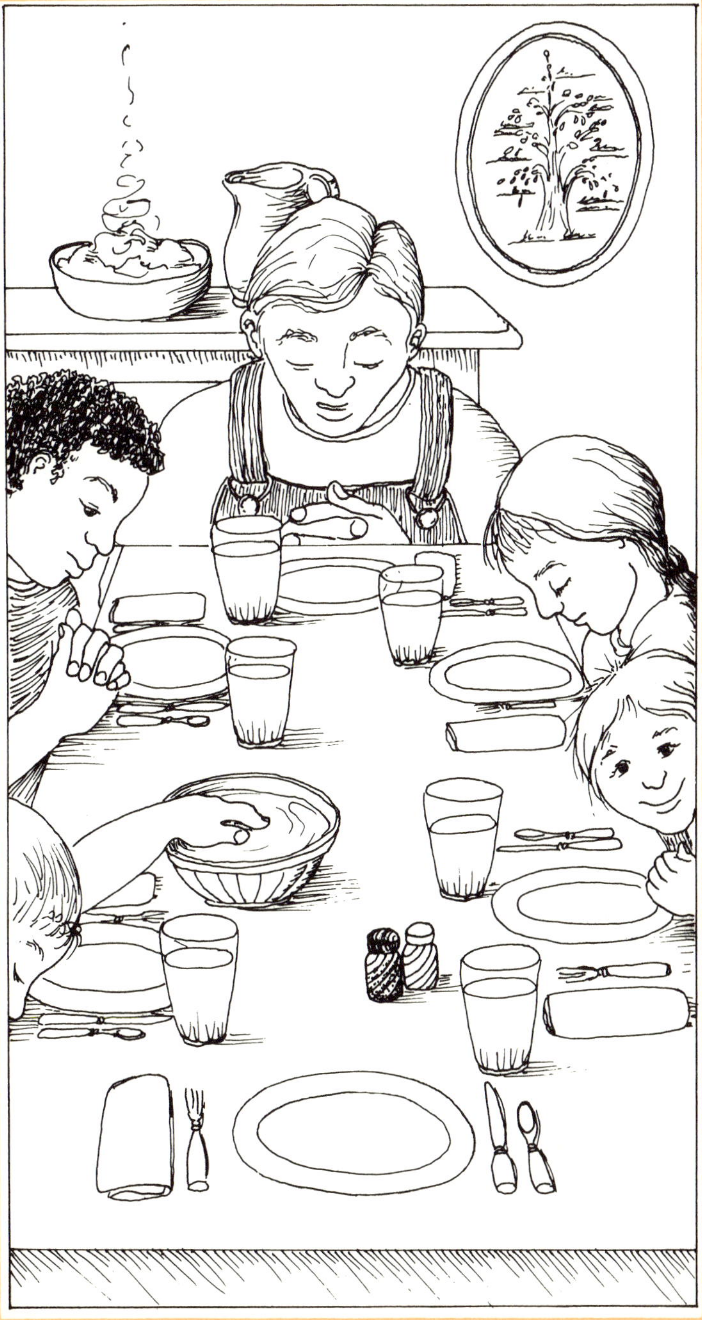

Evening Prayer

I praise you, God, for evening
when shadows grow deep.
And ask you to bless me
as I fall asleep.
Thank you, God.
Amen.

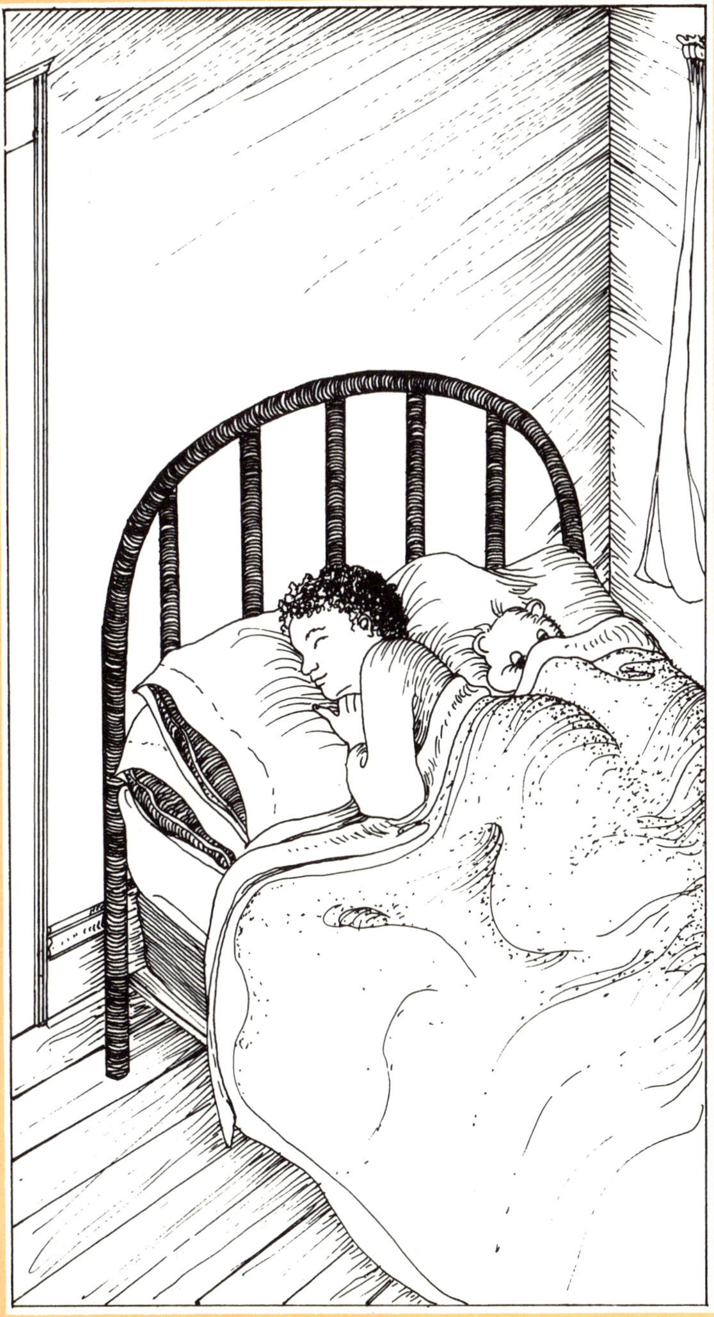

Sunday Song

Each Sunday, God, you gather us
 to listen to your story.
We remember how you love us,
 and we sing about your glory.

We offer thanks for all your gifts
 and your special care.
We praise you most for Jesus
 whose friendship we all share.

We remember how Lord Jesus
 gave himself as friend,
and how he rose on Sunday
 to brand new life again.

We celebrate and share the Lord
 who comes in broken bread;
we share the wine, the cup of life,
 and by them we are fed.

And as our worship's ending,
   before we go our way,
you ask us to share Sunday's joy
   with all we meet each day.

For Sunday shapes all other days
   and fills them with delight.
It gladdens every morning
   and brightens every night.

Then what we do all week long
   — all we see and hear —
we bring it all to Sunday
   to fill the day with cheer.

I thank you, God, for Sunday
   and sing this Sunday song.
I'm one of Sunday's children
   for all the whole week long!

My Own Prayer

_____
_____
_____
_____
_____
_____
_____
_____
_____
_____
_____
_____
_____
_____
_____
_____
_____
_____
_____
_____

Write your own prayer on the lines above.

Draw your favorite way to pray in the frame above.